AFTERLAND

AFTERLAND

POEMS

Mai Der Vang

Graywolf Press

This publication is made possible, in part, by the voters of Minnesota through a Minnesota State Arts Board Operating Support grant, thanks to a legislative appropriation from the arts and cultural heritage fund, and through a grant from the Wells Fargo Foundation. Significant support has also been provided by Target, the McKnight Foundation, the Amazon Literary Partnership, and other generous contributions from foundations, corporations, and individuals. To these organizations and individuals we offer our heartfelt thanks.

Published by Graywolf Press
250 Third Avenue North, Suite 600
Minneapolis, Minnesota 55401

www.graywolfpress.org

Published in the United States of America

ISBN 978-1-55597-770-2

2 4 6 8 9 7 5 3

Library of Congress Control Number: 2016938843

Cover design: Jeenee Lee Design

Cover photo: Matt Black / Magnum Photos

For the ancestors

Contents

AFTERLAND

Another Heaven

I am but atoms
                    Of old passengers

Bereaved to my cloistered bones.

This rotation is my recipe,
The telling of every edition

As a landscape on slow windshields.
The body no longer

                    Baskets fatigue,
No envelope with oxygen left to cure.

When funeral recites
The supper gardens of my forefathers,
Cross-stitch from my mother kin,

                    Then I will come to you

Dressed in my armor of earth,
Ready as you chant my tale.

            When I reach the sloped halls
            And hammock sun,

I won't tell why the split orchid
Falls behind. Instead,
                    I tell why it arrives.

Make me the monarch
morphed from suffering.

Dear Soldier of the Secret War,

Laos, 1975

You once felt the American hand
        that blew its breath
        to drive the fire.

Now they've ended the war.
The American has gone home.

Your Hmong village is a graveyard.

Do you think of your missing wife,
        how the Pathet Lao dragged her

naked, screaming, and bleeding
by her long black hair,

        deep into forest shadows.

        Or your son's head in the rice
        pounder, shell-crumbled.

And your brother, the youngest
who followed you into combat.

It was scalpel that day they captured
        you both. They sliced off
        and boiled his tongue,

        forced it down your throat.

Do you think of the American returning
to the coffee cup,

        new linens
        in a warm bed,

pulling into the driveway.
  Sorry about your mountains,

they say, *here is the last*
     of the ammunition,
     a few cases of grenades.

Do you picture him reading
the morning paper,

   turning on the nightly news.

Maybe you clench your rifle closer,
sling your elegies

to your back,
   hold them as a newborn baby.

You will wait
for hours in ragged fatigues

   with others abandoned
   swarming the dirt runway,

shoving toward the locked
aircraft door

among the scattered shoes,
shirts, blouses, suitcases
   thrown out.

   What grief-song erupts
   when you see the last

American plane take off,
distant above Long Cheng.

How loud do you beg in your gut,

pleading to some invented god
or ancestor or politician:

all of our thousands who died on your side,

> *why won't you authorize*
> *another plane.*

Light from a Burning Citadel

Once this highland was our birthplace. Once
we were children of kings.

Now I am a Siamese rosewood on fire.
I am a skin of sagging curtain.
I am a bone of bullet hole.
I am locked in the ash oven of a forest.

    Peb yog and we will be.

The sky sleeps quilted in a militia of stars.

Someone has folded
gold and silver spirit
money into a thousand tiny boats.

    Peb yog
    hmoob and we will be.

I am hungry as the beggar who cracked
open a coconut to find
the heart of a wild gaur.

    Hmoob and we
    will be.

The tree is more ancient
than its homeland,
shedding its annual citrine
as hourglass dripping honey.

    Peb yeej ib txwm yog
    hmoob.

I dig and dig for no more roots to dig.
I soldier with my severed
legs, my fallen ear.

I've become the shrill
air in a bamboo pipe—the breath
of an army of bells.

Tilting Our Tears on a Pendulum of Salt

You must take the hidden road
For your way
    Out of these bitter woods.

I will go another route.

No more do our nail banks
Lie down in milky water.

        Let us make
        Our separate ways,

Until we meet
Our body's dusty gallery,
Hollow-eyed, until we've

Passed the troops
Who have set our forest table
           With tracheas.

    Our howling knees
Are empty.

Home wages
      Ear-splitting nightmares.

I keep your torn jacket,
Talisman of escape,

Sweetly-clutched as a guava
      From our childhood.

      When I see you again,
We'll build refuge
From newest boughs

      Like the praying mantis
Who sinks into frigid leaves.

Water Grave

We cross under
the midnight shield
and learn that bullets

can curse the air.
A symposium
of endangered stars

evicts itself to
the water. Another
convoy leaves the kiln.

The crowded dead
turn into the earth's
unfolded bed sheet.

We drift near banks,
creatures of the Mekong,
heads bobbing like

ghosts without bodies,
toward the farthest shore.
With every treading

soak, the wading leg,
we beg ourselves to live,
to float the mortared

cartilage and burial
tissue in this river yard
of amputated hearts.

Carry the Beacon

Think of the pause dragged over
                tumultuous days.

You wait and you watch.

But don't linger if a man
                swallows a bomb.

When they burn the olive trees,
                wait a little more.

                Paint yourself with ash
from the last branch.

Wait for the sky to blister outward,
all over.

           The world moves with you
in gradients of orange
and red.

When a far-off noise murmurs
your name, it is the devil disguised
                as a hound.

Ants are spies for the dead.

The cyanide in your left coat pocket.
              Mines have been planted.

           Sometimes your eyes hide
           apparitions.

Sometimes your eyes just hide.

The moon draws close
        you could throw a rock
        and hit it.

Wait for torches to whistle.
        A lasting call.

        The genius moment.

Think of a candle
that goes boom in your chest.

To the Placenta of Return

I buried you after your birth.

     For my son, I placed
You near the central stake,
    Not by the bed.

Soldiers came one day
To steal their offering of men.

With baby, I ran to the forest.

      We hid beneath
        The claret shrubs.

Then his cries, and I pushed
Opium in his mouth.

Now nothing, no sound,
    As I shake here
   In the arms of a liana,

Whisper my crumbs into prayer:

    Birth coat, it won't be long
     Before he re-clothes

In the lit needlework of you.

Clean him, cover him
Toward his way to find
       The old ones.

Yellow Rain

First, the sting
in your nose.

Then in your eyes,
a furnace flared

to hollow
your face.

Flies above
your empty sockets.

Maggots made
your split skin.

Another cow dies
from breathing

as you swallowed
from the same air.

How many days before
it wintered you gray

in this wilderness turned
makeshift graveyard.

How many hours
before the lesions,

before your vomit
hardens the earthen

floor. Somewhere
a house ages cold,

no longer warmed
by the hearth

you once tended.
No one lights

any spirit money.
No one chants the way.

Lima Site 20

Firewood falls from the sky.

Call the mystics to raise the ramparts
　　　　with clandestine men
　　　　whose eyes are fueled by sulfur.

Tell the evergreen's heir,
the calyx creatures
　　　　who give their acoustics to morning,

the library of opaque memory
inside a canefield.
　　　　　　　The verb for neutrality,
　　　　　　　they say,

is to aim covertly.
This is the phantom attack
that never happened, but our fallen know it did.

　　　　　　Tell the weathered architects
of the jungle, limestone
growing inside the cellars.

Wait for the echo to land
before firing the next shot.

　　　　　　To raze the geography
of their ribs, to shred into their names,

tell them I will come back
　　　　as the carved edge of a claw.

Transmigration

Spirit, when I flee this jungle, you must too.
I will take our silver bars, necklace dowry, and the kettle
forged from metal scraps just after the last monsoon.

Among the foliage, we must be ready to see
the half-decayed. You must not run off no matter how much
flesh you smell.

Nor should you wander to chase an old mate.

Spirit, we are in this with each other the way the night geese
in migration need the stars.

When I make the crossing, you must not be taken no matter what
the current gives. When we reach the camp,

there will be thousands like us.
If I make it onto the plane, you must follow me to the roads
and waiting pastures of America.

We will not ride the water today on the shoulders of buffalo
as we used to many years ago, nor will we forage
for the sweetest mangoes.

I am refugee. You are too. Cry, but do not weep.

We walk out the door.

Toward Home

Say a rooster is my mother.
Say there is a coffin in its body

That can only fit my skull.
Say I find a lighthouse burning

In a cave. Smoke above
The field of broken feathers,

I'm flightless, slipping windward
Without a bridge to home.

Say the oven is a bone room.
Say the rock bleeds out

Its boiling eye. I don't know
Where I'm from, but say my feet

Endure because I must have
Come from somewhere.

Say the oryx is a creature
Made of windows. I look inside

Its ear and I see its spirit.
A thousand needles thread

The ends of my hair and
I'm trembling in the storm.

Dear Exile,

Never step back   Never a last
Scent of plumeria

When my parents left
You knew it was for good

    It's a herd of horses never
        To reclaim their   steppes

You became a moth hanging
Down from the sun

Old river   Calling to my mother
Kept spilling out of her lungs

Ridgeline vista closed
Into the locket of their gaze

        It's the Siberian crane
     Forbidden   to fly back after winter

You marbled my father's face
Floated him as stone over the sea

Further   Every minute
Emptying his child years to the land

You crawled back in your bomb

    It's when the banyan must leave
   Relearn to cathedral its roots

Matriarch

She points at the television as if she could translate
Rocky, make sense of Rambo. She is camphor blouse,

Grandmother, keeper of jars for flamed cuppings.
She knows where men have been, those falling into

Tarnished landscapes, sinew machine built from
Fire as if coal were burning their insides. Rocky's arms

Draw skin-drip of diamonds in the meat locker. Rambo
Is carnage cloaked in her homeland mud. She knows

Them as one, their howling stare before they yield,
The way their eyes turn lunar, rogue as dead stars

Thrown back to the graveyard in heaven. In the
Afterwar, there are no more terraces, no more hills,

No hand to sweep the hearth, but always, there remains
A man omitted, and that she knows as well.

Beyond the Backyard

Light passing through
geometry of chain-link gate.
Wig of barbed wire.
                All, I might see.

We pay our rent
to the mechanic next door.
   He's industry too.

Someday,
I will forgive dirt floor
alleys with dumpsters everyone used.

Forgive forklifts
crawling in the lumberyard.

Forgive acoustic winds
lashing open the back door.
                    Anchor let go.

I will climb on the ledge
to peer over,
beggar my eyes
             to a view.

Rusted sedan, wire zipline
to stapled roof, retired
shopping cart missing wheel.

          My parents fled for this.

Sojourn with Snow

That day you brought it home

> *It's like tiny diamonds*
> *That turn to water*
> *Taste like ice Try it*

You too
Once saw how it dropped

A slow searching
Until it went away

Gone are the warm banana leaves
The vapor rains

Evacuee from a rainforest

Hostile frost
Settled your skinny body

Or maybe that city
Would start you over

No layers felt enough

We played with this gift
Every day

Compressed to no more
Numbed in our flushed palms:

Those of refugee children
Who now believed

> *Sprinkle more*
> *In my pile*
> *My footprint stays*

Make me the jasper from
nectar of summer snow.

Original Bones

I wander the earliest days
When I had a written language

Before 1952 when missionaries
In laos wrote one for me

Before 1959 when a phantom script
Came to the *mother of writing*

Before 1986 when I drew
              The letters of mai der

I showed up in southern china
                        A few millennia back
Uncooked people
Led to war

As a child I once looked up
From a farm in fresno's valley

So much deeper the engine echoes
In my kicking eardrum

        Grayer now my eyelids
Gnarl into clouds

There was a time
The mountain came to surrender
            Pressed itself down as my page

The Hour after Stars

Rose petals wash in fire.
I graze my swidden body.

I hear the crow's voice
        before I see it land in the leaves.

A handwritten letter of provision
hides inside
        the pantry.

...

Cold as the wolf
        who takes the calf,
I stare into the boulder's mouth,

make my kills in this citadel season.

I drink from a nest of bees,
sip their stings as ginger
                on my tongue.

...

Afterlife comes at the end
of a book,
        when I walk into the opal winter.

The lines are roped into a ladder.
My dew of blood adjourns.

The latticed coffer closes over
                the little horse.

My Attire Is the Kingdom

Folio of roads
On a hand-woven cape

    Capitol
       To my shoulders

Hem whose pleats
       Are foothills in exile

Every empty space

    Grain walls
Garnish the folds

Linen wraps the leg
Recalls how much I bled

Round patterned copper

       Hair in coils:
Where I stored corn before
Crossing water

Disconnected middle

Silver necklace reminds
Of the iron collar

Quotations braid
Into wool
       Five hundred years:

I wear the mark
    In a belt of coins.

After All Have Gone

I once carried my mollusk tune
All the way to the lottery of gods.

Rain was the old funeral choir
That keened of a hemisphere

Moored under lampwings.
Clouds never left. I knew

The lights would shine clearer
If I closed my eyes, just as

I knew the Pacific would teach
Me to sleep before tying my

Name to the flaming. Here I
Am now at the end of amethyst,

Drizzling another lost sunrise
Inside the quilt of my hand.

Grand Mal

Now that your seizures,
   sage of spells,

has untethered you
from living, we read
once more your story,

a girl who shook the land.

      Touch
where you meant
to speak,
we could never know.

   Wings as monarch
on cheek. Fighter descends,
     hurts to feed
    from knees that
   won't, will be,
never am.

Woman of deep,
     held as love
    thundering home,

here is the coming
of every child lost,

the trembling this moment
of your late stare.

Last Body

I can't leave my hurting skull
Or the rose apple opening inside me.

I'll count the weeks, months,
Unfurling each numbered day in my hair.

Frost ribbons inside my brain,
Canals push up my leg.

I'm moving on
To what the world needs me to know.

I am the angel trapped inside the bullet.
I am the exit wound trapped inside the angel.

Am I the scarecrow
Perched at the end of the human trail.

I'll palm cotton between my prayers
Until the universe has passed,

Waving down jellyfish
To volcano hours.

What force propels a bullet
From its chamber. Is it sourced by water

Trickling in a karst cave,
Or is it an angel's gasp as she flees.

I can't answer it all,
But my mask grows taller every year.

Gray Vestige

From a half-mile, I thought
you were some crust of kelp
and drift. I never could have

guessed it was the last lying
down of you, submitting to
wreckage on this side

of the wind. Dear humpback,
this land is too dry to carry
you further. Soon, you will

be taken, your salty oils,
fragment of sea-frosted spine.
Take every sinew adrift where

barnacles splayed pectoral
fins, your mammal tissue
putrefied into aquatic skin.

Long ago, you were the arched
door into the ocean having
built an orchestra for your

own kind of flight. Some things
return, but never really do.
Like the sifting ground,

the scattered baleen,
and this your body ancient
turned upside down.

Heart Swathing in Late Summer

In the penumbra of an oak under sculpted
Moonlight, we pile the last waking hours

On our faces, breathe the wilderness of dry
Heat waiting for fall ventilations. It feels

Later than it is and the air is already mouthing
The date for tomorrow. At least now, our eyes

Can fall into the craters of a waterproof
Reflection, and we stop for a moment to fill

Ourselves with the kind of light that can only
Be found in the dark. What is night if not for

It being a repetition of unlit squares glued
Jointly, plastered against the thought of midday.

What is not seeing but to echolocate a name.
It's how I find your chin when I can't sense

The meaning of your hands. Weeks ago, it was
Astral rebounds, shiny hinges. We harvested

The fertile Perseids posed recumbent
In the back of a flatbed, tallying the mineral

Opulence reserved for those who wait. Not
Ever so many in return. Now this moon in its

Entirety has never looked so much like
A distant circular kite set ablaze, doused by

The kind of burning a man feels when he hears
The humming of rain against a woman's bare neck.

Meditation of the Lioness

Violets are hatching volcanoes.

Today's bees have swallowed
        The last milk of lanterns.

All the whisper goes out in a drum.
An empire separates inside the nautilus.

On a bed floating the basin,
We fall asleep in fog of the ancients.

By daybreak, we trill
Through cavesongs,

Skate our soles
        Toward the next aurora,

Listen to our fingers
        Kindled as white sage.

Then every cloud is a crib,

Every snowflake a small city
Falling on the eyelash.

Then child, you are cultivated,
Fit to obey
        The balconies inside you.

Now you are free to follow your prey.

Days of '87

You lean by the door before me,
Tall, unshaven, arms at your side,

Oversized duffle by your feet.
I stare at the ironing board, unable

To speak. My fingers unfold the shirt's
collar before trailing it with an iron.

Steam locomotive combing through
A snowy night. Metal tosses vapors.

Mist touches you, then leaves the room.
Five years before, the argument set

You loose. Your father cursed you
From the house on a shining afternoon.

In an hour, he returns from work.
What hangs in the mind, a crumpled

Sleeve, wrinkles stay. Does the mist
Kneel captive to a traveler in a train

Heading toward a salty canyon.
                    Too much has been asked.

A solitary engine, the waiting room,
The feral call.

At Birth I Was Given a Book

I have heard the flames
hunting inside your glossary.

      A starling calls
      from my folded window.

I won't outgrow next year's stone.

Beneath your cordilleras,
exhibit of ripe artery,

      I take my feed, I drink
      my childhood thread.

I find no stamps
in your red lagoon,
      only scent of cypress burning.

They say each birth is given pages
that equals the span of its life.

      Last breath happens
      when last word has been seen.

As if you knew,
long before the war
      where you slept on your kills,

centuries before building
your nation of scars.

You are the pound
of pink cold
    unlocking from the water's spine.

Late Harvest

It started with the apricots
Turning all copper hues on the orchard floor.
The farmer had no one to pick them.

Then oranges.
And the tomatoes.

Someone has tilted the land.

A star flashes
As if it needs help.
Other times it is a loose tooth

In the open mouth of the galaxy.

There are no laborers.
The crates, empty.

Stare long enough at the fields,
The parched horizon,

And you will see, from its lifting,
A kind of smalt fog.

Cipher Song

It's come to this. We hide the stories
on our sleeves, patchwork of cotton veins.

Scribe them on carriers for sleeping
babies, weave our ballads to the sash.

Forge paper from our aprons, and our
bodies will be books. Learn the language

of jackets: the way a pleat commands
a line, the way collars unfold as page,

sign our names in thread. The footprint
of an elephant. Snail's shell. Ram's horn.

When the words burn, all that's left is ash.

Turn me into
starlight lattice,
riding mudwinds at post-thunder.

I Am the Whole Defense

Mid-1700s, Southwestern China

Lightning is the creature who carries a knife.

Two months now,
The rains hold watch.

Statues bury in teak
Smeared with old egret's blood.

I feel the pulse of this inferno,
Tested by the hour to know

That even torches must not waver.

In the garrison, I teach boulders
To trickle from the cliff.

My fallen grow parchment from their hair,

Calligraphy descends
From their lips.

Infantry attack
But my musket knows.

They scale the sides
Yet I tear the rocks.

I am not wife, but my name is Widow.

Let them arrive
To my ready door,
The earth I've already dug.

Diadem on Lined Paper

I saw you first as a man
Whose left arm was the branch of a tree.
Your frail stretch

No thicker than fingers on a gingko,
A body
          Meant for downfall.

Then you turned over
And became a tree
Whose branches were the arms of a queen,

Spanning before me
Like a bridge, earthen silk,
     Consanguinity,

Love that works without a thumb.
I took to you my birth,
My almond song, chrysanthemums

Spun into corona and gold.
Before morning, I gave you
               Memory of blossoms,

Carried your scapular weight.
You learned me, I did not walk
But my feet did.

When fire set itself to expired nights,
I uprooted you from a grave
          To mark my body mourned.

Ear to the Night

I press my hand to your sleep.

        Then I find your spent head under small
whirling tresses

    having digested the clatter
of car horns, children

bustling into sweet shops.

        This might be
the gift of a street:

drumming Saturdays and a Monday palm of heart.

      I've learned that yours
is the chorus of breathing,

a rhythm, forgiving,

that nuzzles the margin within my nature's cratered sigh.

         Once, I felt the feet
of a canyon collapse within you.

Then I come to eyes,
heavy with the tumble of night dew

           having collected verdigris
off the entrance gate.

    Never mind the umbrella
you lost on the subway tracks.

The head is an iron jar filled with many swiveling hours.

All day, I listened,
a city carved

from the hollows of a wire woven shell.

Phantom Talker

You must know
           I am the ghost
    with creosote mouth

hiding behind
           your silent head
    in the vermilion portrait.

My body reduced
to three urns of calories.

        Turn the clutter down,
        saucer, candlestick, doily.

        Can't clear out the deceased
from a secondhand store.

        My sleepwalker
        is amnesia.

To peel an orange
with closed hands,

broke potpourri, sparse-tooth,
           wedding shoes.

Slow pages widow my way.

This Heft upon Your Leaving

I peel to the center for the shape
          of an answer to give you,

          for the way an answer cures
in wet resin

or can hook through the days
toward the pendulous

               blink of your eye.

I answer as air
          answering a clapper

against edges of bronze
before belting out an anthem
of a thousand grazes,

          until I hear paper stones fall
at your softening window.

Years ago, it seemed we were loose
strands swept from our ways,

               two vestigial selves
to hide behind.

          Only the smell darkened when
we washed our hands in a brew
of cardamom and clove,

               and your arms blushed
          over me in earnest.

I tell to your thick listening
as the mouth to a sudden ear,

to your shimmering heat
      as it condenses around me.

      Now what century
fell down at your door?

What cold bowl of oats
did you repurpose into blessings?

From the kettle tongue,
take my answer as a sun-hatched shadow

      slipping to meet your palm
inside the vapor of our moment.

Take this entire autumn of waiting.

Be held by the sense
of an answer

the way an animal can sense
      where the rain will fall.

Final Dispatch from Laos

Concerning our hollow breasts,
Lice factions multiplying in our hair.

Concerning our unused stomachs,
Molars waiting to chew, taste buds

Obsolete. By then, we won't remember
We're alive. We'll be the soil covered

In mines. Concerning last night's
Attack, seven dead, five injured, four

Gone missing, three arms. Concerning
A forest in combat, alliance of trees,

Countercoup to the coup, concerning
Dominos. They'll arrive to collect

Our eyes, but the vines will have eaten
Us up. As for our feet, we left them behind.

And as for our heads, they went foraging
For roots. With regard to shrapnel jutting

From a boy's leg. An old man lured into
The fire by his dream. A woman cradling

Her intestines. With regard to orphans.
A sweet leaf unable to father any *txiv.*

A hand without. We are yet done,
The leftovers ever still waking

Inside the smoke of a hole.

Terminus

I feel the gear switch
               inside the moon.

Touch folded joss paper
    of unburied breath.

I am ready to materialize

              into calf, wrist, ear,
profile whittled from sugar flood.

In a thumb's rotation,
I hear condolences
           from the eclipse,

light the hidden storm in my hands.

I leave on the horse,
             my coral bridge.

Between globe, birth jacket,
    tenant of the flesh,

this is homecoming to a mother
          who will make me.

I the Body of Laos and All My UXOs

It's been forty years of debris
turning stale, and submunitions

still hunt inside the patina of my mud.
I'm stumbling with ankles steeped

in my little wrecked chimneys.
A foot wedged inside a sandal.

The bandage wraps my chest and I
sense the new branches of a cypress

within me, waiting to tear open
the gauze. Where are the high verandas

that once guarded elephants.
What ends the deepening numbers,

resounding into night, a planeload
releases every eight minutes forever.

Left only with cistern walls dismantled
in this era of widows, this is no way

to be lived, clawed and de-veined by
steel splinters concealed. The ground

knows more than a child will ever.
No way to seal the gaps, when a smuggled

climate spills over my body, taints me
with cobwebs spun from overseas.

With Animal

Your mouth opens to glass
that stores late winter,

      meadow within a jar.

I know the brick of your body's roof,

walls unlocking leathered eyes.

You who swallowed the stone
now sleep in your tail's swagger,

       hunt without the jade
inside your marrow.

In these tainted tropics,

you are more, not medicine of teeth
     nor bone that cures.

I will wear your newest splinters,
wake your mask of manna,

mark you as my pendent leg.

Until the crossbow you carry
         rises from

the morning skin's batik.

Ambush

On his knees with a swampy
Cloth, he wipes the ceramic
Crocodile on the bottom shelf.

He won't stand to watch the dust
Crawl too gladly in the light,
Heaping on baseboards,

Up the metal trunk of the desk,
Tired of her pennies elbowed
In crevices, a paper clip

Pushed to the corner as she
Sits in the rolling chair, arms
Folded, smirking like a hyena.

In the mirror, her gaunt eyelids
Slouch, searching for the owner
Of her face. Even a magpie

Can guess its own reflection.
Sometimes the room is a hole,
A chasm digging into their bed.

Below the sofa, a faded receipt
From dinner on Valentine's,
A dusty Post-it that won't unfold,

Price tags from sweaters last
Year. How much dust gathers
In the stuffing of animals.

He hates tangling his feet
On her hair camouflaged
In the rug, stitched in chestnut

Fiber talons. He runs his palm
Along the pelt, scraping the tufts
Into his fist, rip and pull,

Until at last exposed: snout
Piercing through spiked rug,
Built jaws ready to pounce.

A Mouth and Its Name

You told me north water
was not built by virga

but from suicide of the moon.

That letters could turn
        into ruptured atlas,

spill off the brass orbit of a dirge.

Go on living, but never say
the names of the dead.

No muscle inside the bells.
A weapon body does not give.

I mark you in charcoal:
                anonymous.

It was you throwing feet
against the glass frame.

You let me dream of sand rattling
its desert costume,

then polished coins
ripped from a string of iridescent beads.

With it, every shattered hyphen

                that erased you
from your animal sign.

To the Longhorn Hmong

In the dove tree
Corrals of your hair,

A scaffold ascends
     The perfumed winter

Where frost has hewn
    You into azalea.

A cello slinks
From every strand.

     Vineyards ribbon
Inside the intimate air.

    Tonight, the globe
Is so familiar and close.

It could be the cape,
Or a caravan
     Of fossil and wool,

The forebear tresses
Granted to you.

      Every section
Is a calm factory,

A festival of sapphires
     Watering your skin.

Mother of People without Script

You swear the twin spirits
taught you to write.

At night, you climbed
the leaves to hear the gods.

Catch in the throat. Hollow breath.

      Paj is not *pam* is not *pab.*
    Blossom is not blanket is not help.

        Ntug is not *ntuj* is not *ntub.*
      Edge is not sky is not wet.

On sheet of bamboo
with indigo branch.

    To *txiav* is not the *txias.*
       To scissor is not the cold.

The obsidian mask
will make its own sleep,

leave behind the silver
your body won't shed.

Now you are *Niam Ntawv*
who was once a young farmer

scrawling in secret toward
the triggering day.

When they could take no more,
when all that you had was given,

you lined your grave with paper.

When the Mountains Rose beneath Us, We Became the Valley

I won't ask why the saola came
To you, father, or of the poacher who

Followed, but I ask of the country
You lost, the one I never had, unlike

The midwife who sketched birth
Maps on a girl's body and found

A rainforest in her belly. I ask why
A body is born to save money

But can't pay to cross hell's ferry,
Or why snow tells us heaven

Is cold. A sunken missile maddens
Radiant as firework to the eyes

Of a tribesman, witnessing for
The first time. How did an ancient

Boy drown in a homeless river. I ask
Why the warsick warrior who hunts

With claws is hiding a poem. A piece
Of paper hides a garden. What

Harrowed you most arriving at the last
Minute to catch your brother's

Final breath on the hospital bed.
Can a unicorn kindle the night,

Haloed by its flame, torches jutting
From its head. Live on. Ask me how I've

Saved us. Ask me to build our temples
So rooted, so stone, we won't ever die out.

My mouth is nocturnal.

I Shovel into the Heart to Find Its Naked Face

Chambers fall to splinter gravel.
Leaf grows from my throat.

Walls forsake the crumpled ground
It is meant to hold up.

There is much so
A cavity will collect.

I ask to exit from the house:
Spirit of paper temple,
Spirit of cooking fire,

Sentinel at the door, what keeps
Within the loft.

This burns in heaven with
Remembrance of dust:

Spirit of kindling,
Inside the gourd.

My pocket keeps the disfigured
Orange years,
Used wooden
Matches.

I pin myself to the land-living
Slipping surely everborn.

Three

Grave guardian,
slumber with bones from now on.

You are closer to earth
than the reindeer who buries his head

in snow smelling for moss,
nearer than well water,
                    closer than the fox.

Minerals of the living fold into ivy
and basalt. Ground goes on above.

            Drifter of descendants,
let go of your startled skin.

Your pigmented breath
is a frightened thrush
                    prone to bolting.

Do not flee your keeping.

Each plate will be plentiful
as long as the children remember you.

Changemaker,
you are meant to arrive so as to return.

Like arctic fauna
                    shedding winter pelt,
weather dwells inside your mane.

        Lava contours in your palm.

Your throated cold is built from clay
evershifting
            in the hardened eye.

Crash Calling

Do not linger here that is not your brick,

Nor cling to the elbow of a passing car.

The median will trap you during day,

Clip your eyes to hunger as you forage

Along these thin and splintered roads.

        Come to the calico kitchen

Where a grandchild grows and waits

For you to string his failed balloon.

He will drop the thread, every time again,

Until you hear the wishing in his chest.

He will bury the morning dove dying

Inside your shoe. Still, there are secrets

You preserve: tarnished coins folded

In a worn blue cloth.

Thrasher

I murder my tongue,
Hang it on a jagged line

Between the galaxy
Of every bitten wall.

My mother no longer
Hangs the laundry. I burn

My tongue in a tarnished
Truck outside my empty

Yard. A fire at two a.m.
Twenty years ago. The night

Straining a child's wild eyes.
I hide my tongue within

The unleafed wooden scales
Of a tattered eucalyptus.

Grandfather once said
A girl-haunt slept and cried

In its branches. Now she is a
Summit purging into view.

She is the charcoal melody
Gorging the abalone song.

She is the monsoon digesting
The laced agate earth.

I draw back what
The body does not want.

No arms no legs no shape,
She comes blazing out my mouth.

Progeny

              Fire is the child
Whose parents are the dead.

Amid rafters and clay carpet, the body
Learns to pulp.

Night comes in dyads:
       Ravenlight,
     Drumlands.

From now on, I will eat the heartiest
Bamboo, drink from thickest grains

As long as the existing remember me.

Then the great little owl and his half-shut eye,
       Fathermother,
              Canewater.

              Alley sharks invade
The window of my ribs.

       Home is container is memorial.

The Howler

The man howls in my head,
his stony wind

uncoiling in every crevice.

He howls like a sick ghost
plagued by the living.

An aged river of snakes
cascade inside his murky eyes.

He howls like old steam
bolting from an iron pipe.

Like steady illness rising at 2:30 a.m.

Puffs like a cloud in the shape
of a crab at midday.

He blares in my ear like a metal train,
its breath rattling underground.

He howls the clattering deceased,
whose keening voices I hear

in whispers that live,

whose cluttered faces I see
in embers of the book.

Offering the Ox

Before lifted from its lace machine,

        Decimals of incense,
    Shepherd of the finger bells,

Before waking in the after
      As the offspring of a waterfall,

It turns potent as turbine,
Brackets to be reborn.

      Horn to a brook,
Legs into corridor lawn,

It knows how to find the mislaid dead.

    Slight veil turns to azure
Rain intonation on aching bamboo.

Smoke from spirit money
        Rises into canticles.

Blood declines into the silver bowl.

It is the animal basin
With more wrinkles than the horizon,

One braved who gave itself to inherit
      Sleep from the ill.

Dear Shaman,

I'll never smell your mud,
never catch trance though

I've swayed to reveries
by a quivering pine.

Rooster feathers attached to a satellite,
fly out of my prayers.

I've stalked the dead who shake
your curtained eyes. Thrown wax.

A ghost to harden enemy wind.

...

Soulsmith, carve your way
in chorus with quartz.

Instruments guide on all sides
of the sky. Thumb bells rattle drum

split horn egg. Ladder unfolding
as a bridge. I've watched you ride away

on a timber horse to the afterland.
Monsters sprout from gun holes

in people's heads.

...

I cannot look past the prairie to know
what moves inside my nightstand.

But I've dreamt of slipping transparent,
chasing smoke to marry

my spirit's name. I'll know
the ancestors have stopped to rest

when the swallows rise to sing.
I'll know the contour of my home

by every muscle it holds.

...

It's a photograph graying after
each flash. A man falls gossamer

until his face folds away.
He is already at dark's door

when you find him,
crossing the equator's end

without feet or cranium or lung.
Swaying torrent

cannot wash him back.

...

On the day of my birth, you rode
into my tomb. You knew my death

before I could meet my name.
Oracles dismantled

but reassembled like bone puzzle.
In voyage, kin souls came to you.

A murdered uncle tempted you
with tears—

you almost wanted to stay.

Dressing the Departed

The dead cannot be reborn in metal.

Position appliqué under the head.
Fold open its pictured labyrinth

blooming red,
                    gold,
          splitting,
converge,
                    feeding into tributaries

of farmland in the after. Glistening
meadows where buffalo go to graze.

To find the forebears, wear your
kindred ciphers:

poppy shell,
                    stripes,
pinwheel diamond,
                    snail laced on cuff.

Slip on the shoes hand-built from
threads of richest hemp, truest,

only pair ever needed.

Then don the collar embroidered
with fuchsia

          ground stars, for mud health
toward stable seasons.

Put on your tail,
green fringe
     along the bright tipped hat.

Buttons and
silver threads
cannot decay, will postpone rebirth.

Stray organs
are not meant for a body's
                    swamp contents.

When arriving at Root Mother
who sees you wearing

the house she wove
for you at birth,

she will know you then as her own.

In the Swallow's Breath It Is You

I slip into lamb's ear,
Velvet all that I am,

Lung and vein,
Wake open completely

In shell and cotton roots.
These carnelian woods

Clutch me into creature,
My eyelids into armor.

Only there is snow
To tell me why I am here.

I bookend the eventide
With a noctilucent cloud,

A silhouette cradling the era
Of my body's night.

Now firethorn in the garden
Is audience to the winter day,

Listening to the wings
Of a bird for weather,

And this moss, all over, swells
The chamber of your tomb.

Calling the Lost

Hmong people say one's spirit can run off,
Go into hiding underground.

Only the physical stays behind.

To heal, a shaman checks on the spirit
By scraping the earth,
Examining the dirt.

If an ant emerges,
He takes it inside,

Careful not to crush the ant with his hold,
Nor flutter its being into shock
With one exhale.

Sometimes we hide in ants, he says.

He will call for what left
to come back,

and for the found
to never leave.

The Spirit Meal

It's been a hundred years
        since their last morsel.

No honey on palate, they hunt
the living in dreams.

Now the dead come to dine
        in my kitchen.

Paper plates line the floor,
each offering

rice and boiled meat
        from the hen Mother

        butchered in the garage.
Spoons have been dispersed.

        The ground table is set.
As though sounding a dinner bell

in the hereafter, Father chants:
            come eat.

As though they enter in procession
to sit at their chosen plate.

Father pours a shot of rice wine.
Incense fills the air.

        I picture an opened cupboard
in the sky where the feeding hand

        reaches down to find
their waiting mouths.

They trudge as the famished turtle
           whose flaccid head

is ready to break. Grains and poultry
turn molasses on their tongues,

dripping as flame syrup
           off the chin

until their filled liquid faces
                burn away.

Gathering the Last of the Dark

The land has many jaws.
I know not to taste
the vinegar clouds, or walk

barefoot across landmarks
of caterpillars. If I am to
arrive, it will be through

sifting water, through
map of grass and cove.
At the fork that turns

to three, always take
the middle. Storage in my
mind is not my own but those

who save before me.
By now, my fingers ache
too much. I cannot help

the garlic peeler who implores
me to stay and offer my hands
for the shedding. Soon I will

climb the rungs, write my new
provisions. I won't sing just
yet. Crossing virus hillside,

my feet cling heavy
to its shoes. In tall grasses:
fugitive rat, a mask

of leaves, ant possessions.
Lake opens door to another
country. Ear is basement.

I have gone this long
only to discover there are
veins living outside the body.

Your Mountain Lies Down with You

Mourn the poppies, the mangosteen and dragonfruit.

But you come as a refugee, an exile, a body seeking mountains
meaning the same in translation.

Here they are.

Place your palms on the grasslands. Feel the foothills rise
with gray pine and blue oak.

Here, rest not by the lotus of your old country but with
carpenterias and fiddlenecks of spring.

These woodlands may be unfamiliar, their sequoias thicker
than bamboo, and the rains unable to assemble monsoons.

Still, look out to the distance from where you lie.

You will see Mount Whitney is as beautiful as Phou Bia.

The moon is sharp enough to cut your ear as the one from your village.

And notice how these budding magnolias gesture
like the petals on a *dok champa.*

Is that the jungle flower you plucked when you fled, the one you cradled
all the way to the ghettos of St. Paul where you first settled?

You cried every time you saw its picture.

Grandfather, you are not buried in the green mountains of Laos
but here in the Tollhouse hills, earth and heaven to oak gods.

Your highlands have come home,
and now you finally sleep.

My vellum remains.

Afterland

I.

In this settlement of ancestry,

I am myself from the appliqué
of my footprint.

I look toward the wisdom
of sloped hills. There, grandfather
stands under ceiling of thatch.

I dig for my finest blouse, placenta
of my home. It sleeps beneath

the bedpost,
calling as the heartbeat underground.

Great aunt spirit swaddles me with voice of tourmaline.

They come in faces clothed with needlework
of pumpkin seeds.

Ox is landlord to the field.
Mare, my docent story.

II.

More as the lit ear
                    Fiery

                              Tying the animal's call to another

          Voice as chain
                                   As zephyr
                    As sandalwood
                              As psychopomp
                    As snakefur

                              As false ribs
                    As vapored
                         As hung valley
                                   As yellowing

                              As parent pebble
                    As airgonaut
                              As winter cup
                    As fetlock

          Begging all the skins that are lived
          And everything that ever was so deeply tenuous

                    Beg the inside land

III.

In violet night, I wear
heavy mortal eyes,

searching inside corridors
of the rotten lemon grove.

Ferryboat flies
above chestnut plains.

I follow its flag for days.

Land is a vessel
for little hamlets leaning

on hills. Its denizens remember
to swallow their fleeting tunes.

When the market fell into flames,
they learned to play

in the oceanic room
of their empty stomachs.

IV.

To meet the end is to go back
through every dwelling,

return my footfalls
to yesterday's land.

Fresno, California.

Merced, California.

Lansing, Michigan.

St. Paul, Minnesota.

Ban Vinai refugee camp, Thailand.

Long Cheng, Laos.

Sayaboury, Laos.

I go to funerals to meet the ancients.
I go to funerals
to keep.

V.

Drift now as the creature
Not meant to land,

Wings in reverse against wind.
How to index my geography,

Map two miles from inhale to breath.
To recycle the chronology of a clock,

Borrow the ladder
From a shaman's dream:

Once, I lived in the valley.
Then I moved to the tent of ghosts.

Next came partitions of ice.
Metallic roads.

Once, I was born in a bowl.

Notes

In "Light from a Burning Citadel" the Hmong text translates as follows:

"Peb yog" means "We are"

"Peb yog hmoob" means "We are Hmong"

"Peb yeej ib txwm yog hmoob" means "We have always been Hmong"

"Grand Mal" is for Lia Lee.

"I Am the Whole Defense" was inspired by an anecdote from *A Historical, Geographical, and Philosophical View of the Chinese Empire, 1795* by W. Winterbotham, in reference to a Hmong woman who defended a fort by herself after Chinese enemy troops killed all the soldiers, including her husband: "They were conducted into the fort where she had remained alone, and of which she had been the whole defense; sometimes firing her musket, at others tearing off fragments from the rock, which she rolled down on the soldiers who in vain attempted to climb it."

"Diadem on Lined Paper" is a poem based on the art piece *Reina/Madonna* by Mexican folk artist Martín Ramírez.

In "Final Dispatch from Laos" the Hmong word *"txiv"* means both "father" and "fruit" in the Hmong language.

The translation for the Hmong words in "Mother of People without Script" are provided in the poem directly underneath. The phrase *"Niam Ntawv"* literally means "Mother of Paper" and can also mean "Mother of Writing."

Acknowledgments

Unending gratitude to the editors of the following publications in which versions of these poems first appeared:

The Academy of American Poets' Poem-A-Day: "I Am the Whole Defense"
American Poets: "Water Grave" and "Yellow Rain"
Asian American Literary Review: "Lima Site 20," "Dear Exile," "Final Dispatch from Laos," and "Sojourn with Snow" in their special issue commemorating the forty-year anniversary of the Vietnam War
Asian American Literary Review: "Another Heaven," "Thrasher," and "Progeny"
The Boiler: "Diadem on Lined Paper"
California Dreaming: Production and Aesthetics in Asian American Art. An Anthology (forthcoming from the University of Hawaii Press): "Original Bones," "Beyond the Backyard," and "Late Harvest"
The Cincinnati Review: "Cipher Song" and "Toward Home"
The Collagist: "When the Mountains Rose beneath Us, We Became the Valley"
Fairy Tale Review: "The Hour after Stars" and "A Mouth and Its Name"
The Journal: "Matriarch"
The Missouri Review Online: "Light from a Burning Citadel"
The New Republic: "Gray Vestige"
Ninth Letter: "Dear Soldier of the Secret War," and "The Spirit Meal"
Poetry: "After All Have Gone," "Last Body," and "Mother of People without Script"
Radar Poetry: "Meditation of the Lioness," "Three," "At Birth I Was Given a Book," "In the Swallow's Breath It Is You," "Phantom Talker," and "Terminus"
Red Branch Journal: "You've Come Back" (current title of poem is "Days of '87")
Southern Humanities Review: "Offering the Ox"
Stone Highway Review: "Your Mountain Lies Down with You"
The Virginia Quarterly Review: "Heart Swathing in Late Summer," "Ear to the Night," "I Shovel into the Heart to Find Its Naked Face," and "Calling the Lost"
Water~Stone Review: "I the Body of Laos and All My UXOs"
Weave Magazine: "Carry the Beacon"

The task of laboring with words starts with the self but ends in community with others. I am grateful to a number of people who have encouraged me along the way.

First and foremost, an offering of recognition to Carolyn Forché for hearing my voice.

To faculty and friends in the MFA program at Columbia University: Lucie Brock-Broido, Dorothea "Dotty" Lasky, Timothy Donnelly, Mónica de la Torre, Eduardo Corral, Mark Wunderlich, Alice Quinn, Katy Lederer, and all of my workshop colleagues.

To Joseph Legaspi and Burlee Vang who were both generous enough to give my manuscript an initial read.

To Yusef Komunyakaa, an abundance of gratitude.

To the brilliant Jeff Shotts and the incredible team at Graywolf for bringing this book to life.

A million thank yous to the organizations that have supported me on my way: the Academy of American Poets, Hedgebrook, Kundiman, Asian American Writers' Workshop, the Hmong American Writers' Circle, Central California Asian Pacific Women, and last but not least, to all of the young people who touched my life and empowered me during my time at The kNOw Youth Media.

Much love to the community of writers and poets lifting up Fresno and California's Central Valley, including Juan Felipe Herrera, David Mas Masumoto, Lee Herrick, and others. Thank you also to Ellen Bush, MaiKa Yang, and all of the friends, colleagues, and mentors, too many to name, who have supported me through the years.

To my parents, who never once questioned nor doubted my need to write. Thank you for trusting me to do this work. And to my siblings, nieces, and nephews, who remind me to live. I give gratitude to the Cody Family as well.

Finally, to Anthony, my first reader, whose unceasing patience and love saw me through this journey to the afterland and back—this book is yours as much as it is mine.

Born and raised in Fresno, California, Mai Der Vang is the 2016 Walt Whitman Award winner of the Academy of American Poets for *Afterland*. Her poetry has appeared in *American Poets*, the *Cincinnati Review*, the *Journal*, the *New Republic*, *Poetry*, *Southern Humanities Review*, the *Virginia Quarterly Review*, and elsewhere. Her essays have been published in the *New York Times*, the *San Francisco Chronicle*, and the *Washington Post*, among other publications. As an editorial member of the Hmong American Writers' Circle, she is co-editor of *How Do I Begin: A Hmong American Literary Anthology*. Vang has received residencies from Hedgebrook and is a Kundiman fellow. She earned a BA in English from the University of California, Berkeley, and an MFA in Creative Writing from Columbia University.

The text of *Afterland* is set in Arno Pro. Book design by Rachel Holscher. Composition by Bookmobile Design and Digital Publisher Services, Minneapolis, Minnesota. Manufactured by Versa Press on acid-free, 30 percent postconsumer wastepaper.